Dentist Jokes
The Ultimate Collection Of Dental Jokes

Published by Glowworm Press
7 Nuffield Way
Abingdon OX14 1RL
By Chester Croker

Jokes for Dentists

We know that visiting your dentist isn't always a barrel of laughs, and being a dentist can be tough, but we can still give you plenty to smile about. We have many pearls of wisdom to share with you, so brace yourself for plenty of laughs with this bumper collection of dentists jokes.

FOREWORD

When I was asked to write a foreword to this book I was very flattered.

That is until I was told that I was the last resort by the author, Chester Croker, and that everyone else he had approached had said they couldn't do it!

I have known Chester for a number of years and he is a gas. He is an expert at crafting clever puns and amusing gags and I feel he is the ideal man to put together a joke book about our profession – you will find some real pearls inside and very little filling.

He will be glad you have bought this book, as he has an expensive lifestyle to maintain.

Ian Payne

Table of Contents

Chapter 1: Dentist Jokes

If you're looking for funny dentists jokes you've certainly come to the right place.

You won't be feeling down in the mouth after enjoying this collection of the very best dentist jokes and puns around.

This mixture of dentist jokes is a real gas and will prove that dentists have a good sense of humor.

Brace yourself, and let's get going.

Chapter 2: One Liner Dentist Jokes

Be kind to your dentist. He has fillings too.

My dentist seemed distracted when I last visited him; I think he was brushing me off.

Dentists and prison guards have a lot in common. They both have to deal with cavity searches on a daily basis.

As the judge said to the experienced dentist: "Do you swear to pull the tooth, the whole tooth, and nothing but the tooth?"

A great dentist never gets on your nerves.

Contemplating my imminent root canal was deeply unnerving.

My dentist scared me a little when he said, "You don't need to open your mouth any wider. When I pull your tooth, I normally stand outside the room."

I slipped on some toothpaste this morning. I was crestfallen.

I've been to the dentists many times in my life. I know the drill.

My dentist never stops working. He's a compulsive abscessive.

I've finally put my money where my mouth is.

I've got a gold filling.

I got called pretty yesterday and it felt good. Actually, the full sentence was "You're a pretty bad dentist." but I'm choosing to focus on the positive.

Members of the dental profession are the only men who can tell a woman to close her mouth and get away with it.

An orthodontist gets to the root of the problem.

I went to the dentist today, and he seemed rather distracted. I think he was brushing me off.

Dentists are in the rat race too.

They have the same old grind, day after day.

A dentist's favorite book:- "Fifty Shades Of White."

Did you hear about the dentist who planted a garden? Six months later he was picking his teeth.

I got kicked out of the dentist today for using all the nitrous oxide. I am going to have the last laugh though.

Did you hear about the Buddhist who refused a painkilling injection during root canal treatment? He wanted to transcend dental medication.

I went to the dentist without lunch, and he gave me a plate.

A patient asked his dentist if it was a strange feeling having his hands in people's mouths all day to which the dentist replied "I think of it more as me having my hands in their wallets."

My American dentist's favorite song is 'The Yanks are coming.'

My dentist gave my daughter some great advice yesterday. He told her. "Remember, you don't have to brush all your teeth. Just the ones you want to keep."

A best-selling book at my dental school was called "My First Dental Examination" By Hope N. Wide.

Things patients say:-

"My tooth is driving me to extraction."

I said, "Hey, that tooth you pulled wasn't the one I wanted you to pull." The dentist said, "Relax, I'm coming to that one next."

Did you hear about the guy who stole a calendar from the dentists? He got twelve months.

Sign seen on a dentist's waiting room door:- "Open Wide."

Wi-Fi Password sign seen in a dentist's waiting room:- "The wi-fi password is flossdaily – no caps, no spaces."

I went to the dentist today.

He said, "I'm going to put this brace on you as a stop-gap measure."

Sign seen in a dentist's waiting room:- Psalms 81:10 "Open thy mouth wide, and I will fill it."

A book never written, but really should be:- "Pain Management" By Nova Cane.

If dentists make money out of people with bad teeth, why should I trust them and use a toothbrush that 4 out of 5 dentists recommend?

Did you hear about the manicurist and the dentist that couldn't get on with one another? They fought tooth and nail all the time.

I went to the dentist for some root canal work, and I am afraid to say I lost my nerve.

Yesterday, the dentist's wife asked him to pass her lipstick but he passed her a glue stick instead by mistake. She still isn't talking to him.

A dentist friend of mine gave me some great advice, saying I should put something away for a rainy day. I've gone for an umbrella.

A dentist went out for a meal, and when he was asked what he would like for a starter, he said aperitif.

A dentist wanted to buy something nice for his boss, so he bought him a new chair. His boss won't let him plug it in though.

Did you hear about the cross-eyed junior dentist who got sacked because he couldn't see eye to eye with his customers.

Chapter 3: Q&A Dentist Jokes

Q: What is a dentist's office also known as?

A: A filling station.

Q: When do Kings go to their dentist?

A: When it's time to get their teeth crowned.

Q: What's the best time to book a dental appointment?

A: Tooth-Thirty.

Q: What award does the dentist of the year get?

A: A little plaque.

Q: What do you call a Scottish dentist?

A: Phil McCavity.

Q: What game did dentists love to play when they were children?

A: Caps and robbers.

Q: What did the dentist say to the computer?

A: This won't hurt a byte.

Q: What do you call a dentist who doesn't like tea?

A: Denis.

Q: What did one tooth say to the other?

A: Get your cap on; the dentist is taking us out tomorrow.

Q: What is a dentist's favorite movie?

A: Plaque to the future.

Q: Who did the dentist see at the North Pole?

A: A molar bear.

Q: What did the dentist say to the keen golfer?

A: "You have a hole in one."

One for the kiddies:-

Q: Why did the deer need braces?

A: He had buck teeth.

Q: Why did the mobile phone need to visit the dentist?

A: Because it had Bluetooth.

Q: What do dentists call X-Rays?

A: Tooth Pics.

Q: What was the dentist doing in Panama?

A: He was looking for the Root Canal.

Q: Why did the Tooth Fairy go to a psychiatrist?

A: She needed re-assurance that she should believe in herself.

Q: Who has the most dangerous job in Transylvania?

A: Dracula's dentist.

Q: What do you call a dentist's advice?

A: His floss-ophy.

Q: What do you call an old dentist?

A: A bit long in the tooth.

Q: Why does a dentist always seem moody?

A: Because he is always looking down in the mouth.

Q: What did the grizzly bear eat after he'd had his teeth taken out?

A: The dentist.

Q: What did the tooth say to the dentist as he went home for the night?

A: Fill me in next time I see you.

Q: Where does the dentist get his gas from?

A: A filling station.

Q: What does a dentist do on a roller coaster?

A: He braces himself.

Q: What are the six most frightening words in the world?

A: The dentist will see you now.

Q: How many dentists does it take to change a lightbulb?

A: Three. One to administer the anesthetic; one to extract the light bulb and one to offer the socket some pink mouthwash.

Q: Why are dentists like potatoes?

A: Because they are both filling.

Q: Why didn't the dentist ask his secretary out?

A: He was already taking out a tooth.

Q: How are false teeth like stars?

A: They both come out at night.

Q: What's the best thing to put into a pizza?

A: Your teeth.

Q: Why did the blonde go to the dentist?

A: Someone dented her car.

Q: Why was the man told off for looking at sets of dentures in a dentist's window?

A: Because you shouldn't pick your teeth in public.

Q: Why did the doughnut go to the dentist?

A: To get a new filling.

Q: Why is the Tooth Fairy so smart?

A: She has a stack of wisdom teeth.

Q: How did the dentist become a brain surgeon?

A: His drill slipped.

Q: What does a dentist call an astronaut's cavity?

A: A black hole.

Q: How does a student dentist fix a broken tooth?

A: With tooth paste.

Q: What did one tooth say to the other tooth?

A: There's gold in them there fills.

Q: Why did the Queen visit the dentist?

A: To get fitted for a new crown.

Chapter 4: Short Dentist Jokes

A friend of mine set me up with a blind date with a dentist. I took her out for dinner, and at the end of the date she said she had enjoyed herself and that she would like to see me again in six months' time.

This is the one and only knock knock joke in this book, so here goes:-

Knock, knock.

Who's there?

Dishes.

Dishes, who?

Dishes how I talk since I lost my teeth.

Son: "You said that the dentist would be painless, but he wasn't."

Mother: "Did he hurt you then, my boy?"

Son: "No, but he sure screamed out loud when I bit his finger."

A dentist said to his patient "After these cosmetic procedures I am performing you will be like another man."

The patient replied "That sounds great, but make sure you send the bill to the other man."

A teenager asked her dentist "If I give up pizza, chips, popcorn and chocolate, will my braces come off sooner?" to which the dentist replied "Not really. It will just seem longer."

Dentist: "Don't worry. I'm painless."

Patient: "I'm not."

Old man: "Darling, your teeth remind me of the stars"

Old woman: "Is it because they gleam and sparkle?"

Old man: "No, it's because they come out at night."

Customer: "What should I do with all this gold and silver in my mouth?"

Dentist: "Don't smile when you're in a bad neighborhood."

Father: "Do you feel better now that you've been to the dentist?"

Son: "I sure do Dad. He wasn't in."

A man and his wife entered a dentist's office and the husband said to the dental nurse, "I want a tooth taken out. I don't want any gas or any Novocain. I want you to simply pull the tooth as quickly as you can."

The dental nurse said "OK, please show me which tooth is causing the trouble."

The husband turned to his wife and said "OK honey, open your mouth and show the nurse which is the bad tooth."

As soon as the dentist asked the patient to sit down, he pulled out his wallet.

Seeing this the dentist said, "Please don't, you don't need to pay me now."

The patient answered, "Pay you? I just want to count my money before I'm unconscious."

My boss pulled me aside today and said "I thought that you wanted to take yesterday afternoon off to see your dentist. However, I saw you coming out of a restaurant with a friend."

I replied, "Yes, that's right; my dentist is my boyfriend."

A nervous child asked her dentist "Do you extract teeth painlessly?" to which the dentist replied "Not always, just the other day I sprained my wrist and that was painful."

I went to the dentist and he said, "Say Aaah"

I said, "Why?"

He said, "My dog's just died."

"Open wider," The dentist said to his patient.

He then said. "That is the largest cavity I have ever seen, the largest cavity I have ever seen." to which the patient replied, "I'm nervous enough as it is without you repeating something as bad as that."

"I didn't." replied the dentist. "That was the echo."

A guy phoned up her dentist to complain about his bill. "I'm puzzled." he said.

"This is twice the amount that you normally charge."

"Yes, it is," the dentist replied, "but that's' because you screamed so loudly, you scared away my other patient."

Patient: "How much will it cost to have this painful tooth extracted?"

Dentist: "300 dollars."

Patient: "300 bucks for just a few minutes work?"

Dentist: "I can extract it very slowly, if you prefer."

The two main reasons why it's often difficult to solve a redneck murder case.

Firstly, the DNA records all match, and secondly, there are never any dental records.

I went to see where the world's worst dentist was born today. I knew when I found the place. There a plaque on the wall.

Mother: "Has your tooth stopped hurting yet?"

Daughter: "I really don't know. The dentist kept it."

A patient asked his dentist "How much to get my teeth straightened?"

"Fifteen thousand dollars," was the reply.

The patient said "Yikes, it would be cheaper to go to a plastic surgeon and get my mouth bent instead."

I visited the birthplace of the inventor of the toothbrush today. I couldn't find any plaque on the wall at all.

A proud father is showing pictures of his three sons to an old friend and he is asked, "What do your boys do for a living?"

He replied, "Well my youngest is a lawyer and my middle is a neurosurgeon."

"What does the oldest child do?" his friend asked.

The reply came, "He's the dentist that paid for the others' education."

A patient came to his dentist with problems with his teeth and said "I have yellow teeth, what should I do?"

The dentist replied "Try wearing a brown tie."

A patient had severely fractured front teeth as a result of an accident and was discussing a course of treatment with his dentist and he asked him "Before you start, there is one thing I've got to know. Will I be able to play the saxophone when you've finished?"

The dentist replied "Yes, of course you will."

The patient smiled and said "That's great news. I couldn't play a note before."

A guy goes to the dentist with a speech and hearing problem.

The dentist says, "I will try and help, so can you please describe the symptoms to me?"

The guy replies "Yes. Homer is a fat yellow lazy man and his wife Marge has big blue hair."

"Excuse me for a minute," the dentist said to his patient, "but before beginning this work, I must have a drill."

The patient replied, "Do you really need a rehearsal to pull a tooth?"

Two teenage girls are talking and one asks the other "Have you ever come across a guy who, at the slightest touch, made you tremble in every fiber of your being?"

Her friend replied "Yes, my dentist does that to me."

My son was telling me about his experience at a new dentist saying "My teeth are fine but I didn't like the four-letter words the dentist kept using when he was doing a filling."

"What did he say?" I asked.

"Oops" my son replied.

A dentist tells a woman patient that he needs to drill out two of her teeth.

The woman tells him, "I don't like the sound of that; I'd prefer to have a baby." to which the dentist replies, "Please make up your mind madam, as I will have to adjust the chair."

A guy visits his grandmother and his buddy comes along as he has nothing else to do.

While the guy chats to his grandmother, his buddy tucks into a huge bowl of peanuts on the coffee table.

After he has finished them, he thanks the old woman for the peanuts, and she replies "No problem. Ever since I lost my dentures, I can only suck the chocolate off them."

"Did you get your money you are owed?" asked the wife of the dentist who had just returned from his delinquent patient's home.

"Not a penny" complained the dentist, "and to make matters worse, he insulted me, and to top it all he gnashed my teeth at me."

A dentist is late for work and is struggling to find a parking space.

"Lord," he prayed. "I can't stand this. If you open a space up for me, I swear I'll give up drinking."

Suddenly, the clouds part and the sun shines down on an empty parking spot.

Without hesitation, the dentist says: "Never mind Lord, I found one."

"There goes the only woman I only truly ever loved" said the dentist

His assistant asked "Well, why don't you marry her?" to which the dentist replied "I can't afford to. She's my best patient."

A dog walks into a pub, and sits down. He says to the bartender, "I would like a rum and coke please."

The bartender says, "Wow, that's amazing; you should join the circus.'"

The dog replies, "Why? Do they need dentists?"

A dentist in my area went to jail for dealing drugs.

I've been one of his customers for over ten years now, and I had no clue he was a dentist.

A dentist took his cross-eyed bulldog to the vet to be examined.

The vet picked the dog up and said, "Sorry, I'm going to have to put him down."

The dentist said "It's not that bad is it?"

The vet replied, "Nope, he's just very heavy."

I recently attended a meeting of the International Singles Club and I met a German woman who was a dentist.

Unsurprisingly she had perfect teeth, which got me thinking that all dentists from all cultures will probably have perfect teeth too.

So, for my next girlfriend, I am looking for a gynecologist.

One afternoon a dentist asks one of his patients who also happens to be an old friend if he could give out a few very loud screams.

His friend queries the odd request saying "There is no need; the work hasn't been painful."

The dentist tells his friend" It's just that there are so many people in the waiting room right now and I could do with it being cleared out, so I can get home early for once."

Customer: "Why are you laughing?"

Receptionist: "The dentist just pulled one of your teeth out."

Customer: "I don't see anything funny about that."

Receptionist: "It was the wrong tooth."

A retired dentist was walking along the road one day when he came across a frog.

He reached down, picked the frog up, and started to put it in his pocket. As he did so, the frog said, "Kiss me on the lips and I'll turn into a beautiful woman and show you a really good time."

The old dentist carried on putting the frog in his pocket.

The frog said, "Didn't you hear what I said?"

The retired dentist looked at the frog and said, "Yes, but at my age I'd rather have a talking frog."

I read in the local paper that a cannibal dentist was disciplined by his boss.

Apparently, he had been buttering up the customers.

The dentist complained to his friend that his wife didn't satisfy him anymore.

His friend advised he find another woman on the side, and pretty sharpish too.

When they met up a month or so later, the dentist told his friend "I took your advice. I managed to find a woman on the side, yet my wife still doesn't satisfy me!"

A dentist meets up with his blonde girlfriend as she's picking up her car from the mechanic.

"Everything ok with your car now?" he asks.

"Yes, thank goodness," the dipsy blonde replies.

"Weren't you worried the mechanic might try to rip you off?"

"Yes, but he didn't. I was so relieved when he told me that all I needed was blinker fluid!"

I

A young boy was taken to the dentist who told him that he had a cavity that would have to be filled.

The dentist asked him, "What kind of filling would you like for that rotten tooth?"

"Chocolate, please." replied the young lad.

"I came in to make an appointment with the dentist." said the worried guy to the dental receptionist.

"I'm sorry sir, but he is out of the building right now, but..."

"Thank you," interrupted the edgy guy "When will he be out again?"

A young boy was taken to the dentist who told him that he had a cavity that would have to be filled.

The dentist asked him, "What kind of filling would you like for that rotten tooth?"

"Chocolate, please." replied the young lad.

"I came in to make an appointment with the dentist." said the worried guy to the dental receptionist.

"I'm sorry sir, but he is out of the building right now, but..."

"Thank you," interrupted the edgy guy "When will he be out again?"

Chapter 5: Longer Dentist Jokes

A guy and a girl meet one another at a bar. They get along very well and they decide to go back to the guy's place.

After half a bottle of wine, the guy takes off his shirt and then proceeds to wash his hands. He then takes his trousers off and washes his hands again.

The girl says to him, "I bet you're a dentist." The guy, taken aback a little, says "Yes I am, but how did you work that out?" to which the girl replied "Easy - you keep washing your hands."

After they made love the girl said, "You must be a good dentist." The guy was flattered and replied, "Yes I am a good dentist, but how did you work that out?"

The girl replied, "I didn't feel a thing."

A dentist tells his mature patient a tooth has to come out, and that he will need to give him a shot of Novocain, but the patient grabs hold of the dentist's arm and declares "No. I hate needles. I really do not want an injection."

The dentist replies "Ok, fine we'll go with gas then."

The patient replies "No. Last time I had gas I was nauseous for days afterwards."

The dentist reaches into the medicine cabinet, and offers the patient a Viagra pill.

The patient looks surprised and asks "Will that kill the pain?"

"No," replies the dentist, "but it will help give you something to hold onto to while I pull out the tooth!"

A guy asks the dental nurse how much it will cost to extract two wisdom teeth.

"Three hundred dollars", says the nurse.

The guy complains, "That's an astonishing amount of money; is there a cheaper way of doing it?"

"Well," the nurse replies, "If you choose not to have anaesthetic, I can reduce the price to two hundred dollars."

The guy says, "That's still too much, is there an alternative?"

"Well", says the nurse "if we omit the anesthetic and we just rip the teeth out with a pair of pliers, we can do it for one hundred dollars."

The guy says, "No, it's still too expensive."

"Well", says the nurse, "if I let our new student dentist do it, as it's about time he did his first extraction with a pair of pliers, I suppose I can reduce the price to fifty dollars."

"Fantastic." says the guy, "Book my wife in for next Thursday morning."

A young dentist is sitting at the bar after work one night, when a burly sweaty construction worker sits down next to him.

They start talking and eventually the conversation moves on to nuclear war.

The dentist asks the construction worker, "If you hear the sirens go off, the missiles are on their way, and you've got just 15 minutes left to live, what would you do?"

The construction worker replies, "I'm going to jump on anything that moves."

The construction worker then asks the dentist what he would do to which he replies, "I'm going to keep perfectly still."

A male dentist was talking to two of his buddies about their daughters.

The first friend says "I was cleaning my daughter's room the other day and I found a pack of cigarettes. I didn't even know she smoked."

The second friend says, "That's nothing. I was cleaning my daughter's room the other day and I found a half full bottle of Vodka. I didn't even know she drank."

The dentist says, "That's nothing. I was cleaning my daughter's room the other day and I found a pack of condoms. I didn't even know she had a penis."

On Monday morning I told my boss I had a dentist appointment later that day, and I asked to leave at 2pm and told him I would make the time up later in the week.

He said, "That's fine; no problem."

On Friday afternoon, he came up to me and asked, "How come you put on your timesheet that you finished at 5pm on Monday – you went to the dentist at 2pm."

I replied, "I told you I'd make it up."

Carlo the property developer and his dentist pal buddy Doug, went bar-hopping every week together, and every week Carlo would go home with a new woman while Doug went home alone.

One week Doug asked Carlo his secret to picking up women.

"Well," said Carlo "When she asks you what you do for a living, don't tell her you're a dentist. Tell her you're a lawyer."

Later Doug is dancing with a woman when she leans in and asks him what he does for work. "I'm a lawyer," replies Doug.

The woman smiles and seductively asks, "Want to go back to my place? It's not far away."

They go to her place, have some fun and an hour later, Doug is back in the pub telling Carlo about his success.

"I've only been a lawyer for an hour," Doug snickered, "And I've already screwed someone!"

A shy six-year old girl was at the dentist for her first check-up and cleaning. The dental hygienist tried to strike up a conversation with her, but got no response.

After the cleaning was completed, the dentist did the check-up. He, too, tried to strike up a conversation with the little girl and also received no response.

"Do you know how old you are?" the dentist asked her, and the little girl immediately held up six fingers.

"Oh, I see," replied the dentist, "and do you know how old that is?" Once again, the little girl held up six fingers.

The dentist asked, "Can't you talk little girl?"

With an annoyed look, the little girl replied, "Can't you count a**hole?"

A dentist, a carpenter and an electrician were chatting about what prank to pull on a mutual friend who was getting married.

The electrician said "I will wire up the bed so that when our buddy and his new bride sit on it, they'll get a small electric shock."

The carpenter said "I will rig the bed so that when they get shocked and jump apart, the bed will simply collapse."

The dentist just said "Let me think about what I can do."

After their buddy's wedding, the groom sent an email from their honeymoon destination which said "When we both sat on the bed and got a shock, we had to laugh. When the bed fell apart, we had to laugh again, but just whose idea was it to put Novocain in the Vaseline?"

A man went to his dentist and after a thorough examination, the dentist told him, "The upper plate I put in for you eight months ago is wearing away. What have you been eating that could possibly cause that?"

The man replies, "About six months ago my wife made a delicious soy sauce to put on the meal we were having for dinner. I loved it so much she now makes it very week, and I now put it on pretty well everything meat, fish, vegetables; you name it."

The dentist then said, "That is probably what has caused the problem. Soy sauce has lots of salt in it, which is very corrosive, and it is eaten away your upper plate. I recommend that I make you a new plate, but this time I will use chrome."

"Why chrome?" asked the patient to which the dentist replied, "It's simple really - there's no plate like chrome."

Ron is talking to two of his friends, Jim and Shamus.

Jim says, "I think my wife is having an affair with a dentist. The other day I came home and found some dental forceps under our bed."

Shamus then confides, "Me too! I think my wife is having an affair with an electrician. The other day I found some wire cutters under our bed."

Ron thinks for a minute and then says, "You know - I think my wife is having an affair with a horse."

Both Jim and Shamus look at him in complete disbelief.

Ron sees them looking at him and says, "No, seriously. The other day I came home early and I found a jockey under our bed."

A group of dentists, all aged 40, discussed where they should meet for a reunion lunch. They agreed they would meet at a place called The Dog House because the barmaids had big breasts and wore short-skirts.

Ten years later, at age 50, the dentists once again discussed where they should meet for lunch.

It was agreed that they would meet at The Dog House because the food and service was good and there was an excellent beer selection.

Ten years later, at age 60, the friends again discussed where they should meet for lunch.

It was agreed that they would meet at The Dog House because there were plenty of parking spaces, they could dine in peace and quiet, and it was good value for money.

Ten years later, at age 70, the friends discussed where they should meet for lunch.

It was agreed that they would meet at The Dog House because the restaurant was wheelchair accessible and had a toilet for the disabled.

Ten years later, at age 80, the dentists, now all retired, discussed where they should meet for lunch.

Finally it was agreed that they would meet at The Dog House because they had never been there before.

Chapter 6: Dentist Pick-Up Lines

Hello there, it looks like you've got a hole that needs filling.

Why don't you lie back and let me fill your cavities.

Stick your tongue out farther for me.

I wish you were my teeth, so I could grind you in my sleep.

I'll bring a smile to your face.

Be with me and you can be struck by whitening.

You're so sweet I'm getting a toothache just looking at you.

I'm a dentist - it's my job to put it in your mouth.

You're real eye candy and I have got a sweet tooth.

I'd like to drill you and fill you.

You're so sweet I'm getting cavities.

I'd like to rinse and repeat with you.

Did you know that semen contains zinc and calcium, both of which are proven to prevent tooth decay.

I would like to punch you in the mouth with my own mouth - very softly.

If you were a tooth, you would be an upper left lateral incisor.

If you were a polishing disc, you'd be superfine.

Lie back and let me do a detailed cavity search.

Chapter 7: Bumper Stickers for Dentists

I've got 99 problems but my teeth ain't one of them.

I hate being sexy but I'm a dentist so I can't help it.

And on the eighth day God created dentist.

Dentists have fillings too.

Molar power.

You can't handle the tooth.

Expect the whole tooth and nothing but the tooth.

We'll do our Crest.

Struck by whitening.

Bend over and floss.

Dentists do it twice a day.

Rinse and spit.

Flossy Posse.

Gum Getters.

Whitening Lightning.

On Retainer.

Nothing but the Tooth.

Plaque Attack.

About the Author

Chester Croker has written many joke books and was voted Comedy Writer Of The Year by the International Jokers Guild. Chester is known to his friends as Chester the Jester and this book is a result of him spending many hours in dentists' chairs dreaming up jokes as he finds the chairs weirdly relaxing places to be.

If you see anything wrong, or you have a gag you would like to see included in the next edition of this book, please message us via the glowwormpress.com website.

If you did enjoy the book, kindly leave a review on Amazon so that other dentists can have a good laugh too.

Thanks in advance.

Made in the USA
Middletown, DE
11 December 2020